What *Babies* Teach Us

What *Babies* Teach Us

*Life's Lessons Learned
From the Small & Sweet*

Willow Creek Press

Editor: Andrea Donner

Photo Credits

© **Peter Arnold, Inc.**: p.2 © Bart Harris; p.9 © Eberhard Grames/Bilderberg; p.13 © Richard Hirneisen;
p.14 © Laura Dwight; p.17 © Angelika Jakob/Bilderberg; p.21 © Angelika Jakob/Bilderberg;
p.25 © Richard Hirneisen; p.26 © Angelika Jakob/Bilderberg; p.53 © John Greim; p.82 © Richard Hirneisen;
p.86 © Richard Hirneisen; p.89 © Frieder Blickle/Bilderberg; p.93 © Richard Hirneisen

© **Norvia Behling**: pages 30, 41, 81, 96

© **The Image Finders**: p.33 © Mark E. Gibson; p.37 © Novastock; p.78 © Eric Berndt;
p.94 © Mark E. Gibson

© **Barbara Peacock / www.barbarapeacock.com**: pages 6, 29, 45, 46, 49, 57, 61, 62, 65, 66, 69, 77, 91

© **Terry Wild Studio, Inc.**: pages 10, 18, 22, 35, 38, 42, 50, 54, 58, 70, 73, 74, 85

Printed in Canada

For Jeremy and Tracy

Having a child is surely the most beautifully irrational
act that two people in love can commit.

Bill Cosby

adventure

Motherhood is like Albania—
you can't trust the brochures; you have to go there.

Mami Jackson

I don't know why they say, "You have a baby."
The baby has you.

Gallagher

a m a z e m e n t

We find delight in the beauty and happiness of children
that makes the heart too big for the body.

Ralph Waldo Emerson

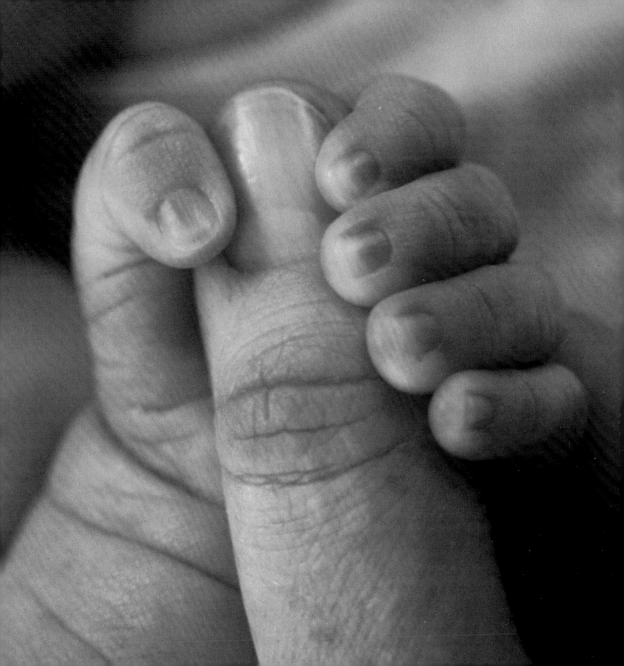

Children have never been very good at listening to their elders,
but they have never failed to imitate them.

James Baldwin

amusement

A child is a most desirable pest.

Max Gramlich

Babies are such a nice way to start people.

Don Herold

appreciation

If one feels the need of something grand, something infinite,
something that makes one feel aware of God, one need not
go far to find it. I think that I see something deeper, more infinite,
more eternal than the ocean in the eyes of a little baby...

Vincent Van Gogh

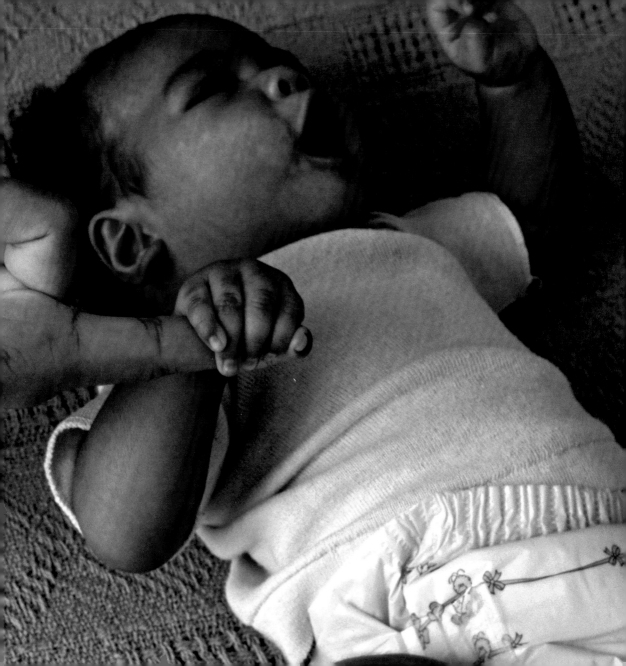

A babe in the house is a well-spring of pleasure, a messenger of peace and love, a resting place for innocence on earth, a link between angels and men.

Martin Fraquhar Tupper

awareness

What greater thing is there for human souls than to feel that they are joined for life—to be with each other in silent unspeakable memories.

George Eliot

Making the decision to have a child is momentous.
It is to decide forever to have your heart go
walking around outside your body.

Elizabeth Stone

a w e

Every baby born into the world is a finer one than the last.

Charles Dickens

We can do no great things; only small things with great love.

Mother Teresa

benevolence

Father asked us what was God's noblest work. Anna said men, but I said babies. Men are often bad, but babies never are.

Louisa May Alcott

We will never know the love of our parents for us
till we have become parents.

Henry Ward Beecher

caring

Before you were conceived I wanted you.
Before you were born I loved you.
Before you were here an hour I would die for you.
This is the miracle of love.

Maureen Hawkins

You can't plan the kind of deep love that results from having children.

Unknown

compassion

As parents, we never stand so tall as when we stoop to help our children.

Dr. Anthony P. Witham

A mother's children are portraits of herself.

Unknown

c o n t e n t m e n t

*In the sheltered simplicity of the first days after a baby
is born, one sees again the magical closed circle, the miraculous
sense of two people existing only for each other, the tranquil sky
reflected on the face of the mother nursing her child.*

Anne Morrow Lindbergh

It was the tiniest thing I ever decided to put my whole life into.

Terri Guillemets

dedication

I looked on child rearing not only as work of love and duty
but as a profession that was fully interesting and challenging
as any honorable profession in the world, and one
that demanded the best that I could bring it.

Rose Kennedy

Little children are still the symbol of the eternal
marriage between love and duty.

George Eliot Romola

devotion

Never fear spoiling children by making them too happy.
Happiness is the atmosphere in which all good affections grow.

Thomas Bray

There is a power that comes to women when they give birth.
They don't ask for it; it simply invades them. Accumulates like
clouds on the horizon and passes through, carrying the child with it.

Sheryl Feldman

empowerment

Anyone who thinks women are the weaker sex
never witnessed childbirth.

Unknown

A father carries pictures where his money used to be.

Unknown

financial management

The joy of having a baby can be expressed
in two words: tax deduction.

Unknown

Babies fill a hole in your heart you never new existed.

Unknown

fulfillment

Time becomes frozen as woman by woman, birth by birth
They're all connected through their bodies & songs
It knows no boundaries, no color, no races
It fills all their bodies, their hearts, their faces
The sounds of each woman as she sings the Birthsong.

Maya Angelou

No animal is so inexhaustible as an excited infant.

Amy Leslie

f u n

Where children are, there is the golden age.

Novalis

The guys who fear becoming fathers don't understand
that fathering is not something perfect men do,
but something that perfects the man. The end product
of raising a child is not the child, but the parent.

Frank Pittman

g e n t l e n e s s

There is nothing stronger in the world than gentleness.

Han Suyin

The simplest toy, one which even the youngest child

can operate, is called a grandparent.

Sam Levenson

grandparenting

The birth of a grandchild is like the arrival of spring,

awakening from a deep winter's sleep and budding forth

with new life, bringing joy and optimism for the future.

Vera Allen-Smith

Looking at people who belong to us, we see
the past, present, and future.

Gail Lumet Buckley

heritage

The history of our grandparents is remembered not with rose petals but in the laughter and tears of their children and their children's children. It is into us that the lives of grandparents have gone. It is in us that their history becomes a future.

Charles and Ann Morse

A baby is God's opinion that the world should go on.

Carl Sandburg

hope

Babies are always more trouble than you thought—
and more wonderful.

Charles Osgood

A man finds out what is meant by a "spitting image"
when he tries to feed cereal to his infant.

Imogene Fey

humor

A perfect example of minority rule is a baby in the house.

Unknown

The young and the old are closest to life.
They love every minute dearly.

Chief Dan George

j o y

Of all the joys that brighten suffering earth,
what joy is welcomed like a new-born child?

Lady Caroline Sheridan Norton

Kind words can be short and easy to speak,
but their echoes are truly endless.

Mother Teresa

kindness

Speak tenderly to them. Let there be kindness
in your face, in your eyes, in your smile.
Don't only give your care, but give your heart as well.

Mother Teresa

Laughter is like changing a baby's diapers. It doesn't permanently solve any problems, but it makes things more acceptable for a while.

Unknown

laughter

No day can be so sacred but that the laugh of a little child will make it holier still.

Robert Green Ingersoll

When you look at your life, the greatest happinesses are family happinesses.

Dr. Joyce Brothers

maturity

A real family man is one who can look at his new child as an addition rather than a deduction.

Unknown

The moment a child is born, the mother is also born.
She never existed before. The woman existed, but the mother, never.
A mother is something absolutely new.

Bhagwan Shree Rajneesh

parenting

Fatherhood is the most creative, complicated, fulfilling, frustrating,
engrossing, enriching, depleting endeavor of a man's adult life.

Kyle D. Pruett

You can learn many things from children.
How much patience you have, for instance.

Franklin P. Jones

patience

If the very old will remember, the very young will listen.

Chief Dan George

Who is getting more pleasure from this rocking,
the baby or me?

Nancy Thayer

peacefulness

Time spent with your family doing ordinary things
is the most extraordinary time of all.

Jan Blaustone

In raising my children I have lost
my mind but found my soul.

Unknown

perspective

The best things in life aren't things.

Unknown

You will always be your child's favorite toy.

Vicki Lansky

playfulness

You should study not only that you become a mother when your child is born, but also that you become a child.

Dogen

There is only one pretty child in the world,

and every mother has it.

Chinese proverb

pride

Don't take up a man's time talking about the

smartness of your children; he wants to talk to you

about the smartness of his children.

Edgar Watson Howe

The watchful mother tarries nigh,
though sleep has closed her infant's eyes.

John Keble

protectiveness

Home is where a father's strength
Surrounds, protects his own . . .

Anna Vallance

Love is just a word until someone comes along
and gives it meaning.

Unknown

purpose

Perhaps the greatest social service that can be rendered by
anybody to the country and to mankind is to bring up a family.

George Bernard Shaw

True, a mother has many cares, but they are sweet cares.

John Welch Dulles

responsibility

For the mother is and must be, whether she knows it or not,
the greatest, strongest and most lasting teacher her children have.

Hannah Whitall Smith

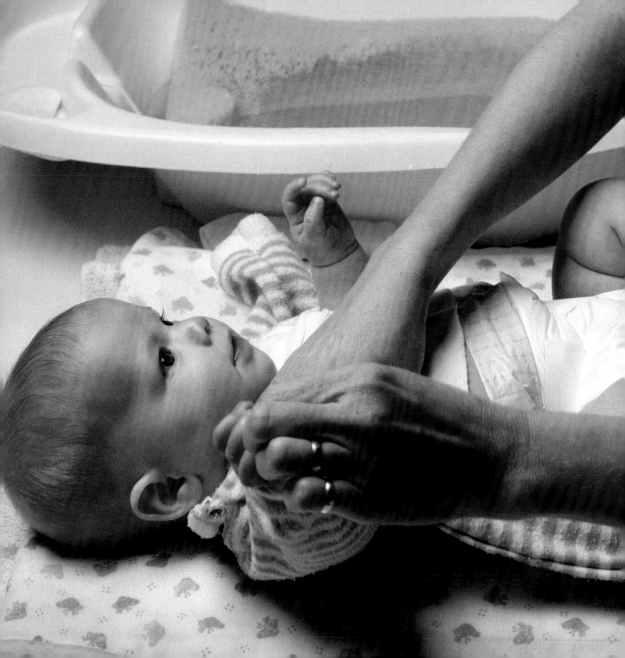

A happy childhood is one of the best gifts that parents have in their power to bestow.

R. Cholmondeley

selflessness

Love is, above all else, the gift of oneself.

Jean Anouilh

When babies look beyond you and giggle,
maybe they're seeing angels.

The Angel's Little Instruction Book

silliness

A child is a curly, dimpled lunatic.

Ralph Waldo Emerson

There never was a child so lovely but his mother

was glad to get him asleep.

Ralph Waldo Emerson

s l e e p l e s s n e s s

People who say they sleep like a baby usually don't have one.

Leo J. Burke

Who is not attracted by bright and pleasant children,
to prattle, to creep, and to play with them?

Epictetus

sweetness

Children remind us to treasure the smallest gifts,
even in the most difficult of times.

Allen Klein

Women know a simple, merry, tender knack of tying sashes,
fitting baby shoes, and stringing pretty words that make
no sense. And kissing full sense into empty words.

Elizabeth Barrett Browning

tenderness

A child's hand in yours—what tenderness and power it arouses.

Marjorie Holmes

Hold your child's hand now, while you still can.

Unknown

thankfulness

If I had my life to live over, instead of wishing away nine months of pregnancy, I'd have cherished every moment and realized that the wonderment growing inside of me was the only chance in life to assist God in a miracle.

Erma Bombeck

Children are love made visible.

American proverb

true love

*I love these little people; and it is not a slight thing
when they, who are so fresh from God, love us.*

Charles Dickens

We may find some of our best friends in our own blood.

Ralph Waldo Emerson

t r u s t

You're welcome.
That no matter who you are,
You're loved.
Welcome.

Rita Ramsey

A mother's love endures through all.

Washington Irving

unconditional love

A father's love warms the hearts of his children forever.

Unknown

That first little cry is mightier than
the cheers of ten thousand people.

Unknown

understanding

A baby will make love stronger, days shorter, nights longer,
bankroll smaller, home happier, clothes shabbier,
the past forgotten, and the future worth living.

Unknown

Life has loveliness to sell…
children's faces looking up
holding wonder like a cup.

Sara Teasdale

wonder

A new baby is like the beginning of all things—
wonder, hope, a dream of possibilities.

Eda J. Le Shan